Effective Meditations
for the Offering
and Communion

Effective Meditations for the Offering and Communion

Elmer B. Fuller

Writers Club Press
San Jose New York Lincoln Shanghai

Effective Meditations for the Offering and Communion
All Rights Reserved © 2000 by Elmer B. Fuller

Writers Club Press
an imprint of iUniverse.com, Inc.

For information address:
iUniverse.com, Inc.
5220 S 16th, Ste. 200
Lincoln, NE 68512
www.iuniverse.com

Scripture taken from the HOLY BIBLE,
NEW INTERNATIONAL VERSION.
Copyright © 1973, 1978, 1984 International Bible Society.
Used by permission of Zondervan Bible Publishers.

ISBN: 0-595-15194-9

Printed in the United States of America

Dedicated to those in Abilene, Mexico, Benzie, and Farmington who focused my attention each Sunday upon the offering and communion

The more the words, the less the meaning,
and how does that profit anyone?

Ecclesiastes 6:11

CONTENTS

PREFACE

This book evolved from a simple idea. I was driving home from a meeting, listening to a cassette tape by John Maxwell. Maxwell's message convinced me to improve the teaching of stewardship at my church. As a result I began to build a list of Scriptures and ideas for offering meditations. Our church always had a prayer before the offering, but only occasionally had a meditation. I wanted to establish the offering meditation. The list would help those who gave it. A list of ideas, how simple!

As I built the list, I thought I should also build a list for communion meditations, and the project grew.

Later I thought about our occasional need to train new people to deliver meditations. I decided to include tips on writing and delivering meditations. And the project grew still larger.

Over the next year the book continued to develop. Ready-to-use meditations and other features were added.

I believe that meditations for the offering and communion are important. They set the stage for these worship events. The quality of the meditation has a direct effect upon the quality of worship church members experience. Effective meditations enhance this worship. Bad meditations can totally disrupt it.

My dream in this book is to help you deliver effective meditations so the people in your church will experience excellent worship of God.

ACKNOWLEDGEMENTS

A special word of thanks goes to Lloyd Pelfrey who offered many helpful suggestions and corrections and to Elaine, my wife, who proofread the manuscript and encouraged me.

The illustration of the father and son buying french fries, which is used in the chapter *Stories Are Good*, is adapted from an audio cassette from *Proven Principles for Successful Stewardship* by John Maxwell.

INTRODUCTION

CONSIDER THE RINGMASTER'S ART

The spotlight circles the tall man in the red coat and black top hat. "Ladies and gentlemen, in the center ring you will witness a spectacle of death-defying mastery over the king of beasts!"

A circus captures the thrill of childhood in each of us. We marvel at acrobats, lion-tamers and sword-swallowers. We laugh at clowns and delight in cotton candy. Each act brings a new thrill.

Consider for a moment the ringmaster. No one really comes to see him. No one comments when leaving, "Wow! What a great ringmaster!" We hardly remember him, but his job is crucial to our enjoyment. The ringmaster is not the show. *He focuses our attention on the show.* He helps move our attention from act to act, weaving a seamless sense of wonder.

Delivering offering and communion meditations is much the same. Those who deliver them focus attention upon the "real show"—an act of worship. In fact, they are more crucial to worship than a ringmaster is to a circus. Worship is far more important than entertainment. If people don't watch entertainment, what have they lost? But if they fail to worship, both God and the worshipers are cheated.

The art of delivering meditations is the art of the ringmaster. Done correctly, it focuses the congregation upon God. Their minds will not wander, but they will anticipate the offering or communion with a seamless sense of wonder.

This book will develop the art in you. Whether you give meditations each week, or have never given one, this book will help you prepare and deliver *good* meditations. It is divided into several parts to help with each aspect of the art of effective meditations. The next chapter will explain which part of the book can help with a specific task.

But the book possesses a secret. It is written in bite-sized chunks of information, just like a good meditation. By reading it you will absorb this style as well as receive instruction in it.

Remember our purpose: direct attention on what comes next.

HOW TO USE THIS BOOK

This book is divided into several sections.

In a hurry? Do you need a meditation, but don't have much time? Find a meditation in the *Ready-To-Use Offering Meditations* or the *Ready-To-Use Communion Meditations* sections.

Do you need some tips on how to deliver meditations? Consult the chapter on *Delivering Meditations.*

Do you need starter ideas for a meditation? Dig through the dozens of suggestions in the *Ideas for Offering Meditations* and the *Ideas for Communion Meditation* sections. Be sure to read the tips on using the ideas at the beginning of the section.

Want to make your meditations effective and dynamic? Study the chapters in the *How to Make Meditations Good* section and apply what you learn.

Need quick instruction on how to create an effective mediation? See the *Recipe for a Good Meditations.*

Want more details on writing meditations? Read the chapters on *Writing Meditations* and *Customizing Meditations.*

Have you selected a verse of Scripture? Use the *Index of Scriptures* to find suggestions for the verse.

Do you have some meditation ideas you want to save? Jot them on the blank pages at the back of the book.

"Why aren't there more ready-to-use meditations in the book?" The best meditations use stories from your personal experience. That's why most of the starter ideas in the *Ideas* sections prompt you to think of personal experiences that can be combined with the Scripture. You are the key to effective meditations.

What Makes a Meditation Good

SHORT IS GOOD

"I want to introduce to you, John Livingston, who will be our speaker today. You know, John and I go back a long way. I'd like to tell you a story about John. You see, you may not know this, but...[blah]...[blah]...[blah]..."

Surely you have cringed inwardly when someone introduced a speaker with lengthy details. I've attended service clubs, workshops, and even church services in which the person introducing the speaker abused his or her role. Some have "introduced" for five minutes, sometimes even ten. I inwardly want to stand and say, "Enough already! We want to hear the speaker, not you!"

By delivering a meditation, we introduce the next section of a worship service. **A good meditation is short and to the point.** Some of the best offering meditations I have ever heard lasted less than a minute. They captured my attention and prepared me to worship through the offering.

Most churches have a schedule and time restrictions for the worship service. The time allotted for a meditation may be as short as 90 seconds. It is imperative that the meditation begin and end on time. Even in churches with more flexible limits, the effective length of the meditation is determined by the attention span of the audience.

3

Three minutes is the maximum length a meditation should be. A three-minute meditation contains ample time to focus people upon the worship event.

Worship is a combination of attitude and action. A good meditation focuses attention and sets the attitude for the action of worship. An example follows. Time yourself as you read it aloud.

2 Corinthians 9:7 says, "Each man should give what he has decided in his heart to give, not reluctantly or under compulsion, for God loves a cheerful giver."

One of the most cheerful people I know is John Thybault. John and his wife lived across the hall in our college apartment building. I loved to talk to John! He always smiled and seemed happy to see me. He had enthusiasm for life.

Several times John and his wife babysat an infant with colic. The poor child never seemed happy. It cried constantly. We could hear the crying in our apartment. Nobody likes to hear babies cry. We'd rather hear them laugh.

As you give your offering today, what should your attitude be? Don't be a crybaby. Don't give reluctantly. As you place your gift into the offering, smile! Bring cheerfulness to God, not just your money. God loves a cheerful giver.

Rambling Is Bad

"Ladies and gentlemen, in the center ring you will witness a spectacle of death-defying mastery over the king of beasts. Watch Bruno the Magnificent stick his head into the gaping jaws of a hungry lion! Bruno learned his skills at the Circus College in Florida in 1998. He also studied whip cracking and chair holding. Of course, the real secret is to dominate the animal. One must never show fear. Titus, the male, five-year-old African lion has six-inch teeth and bad breath. Titus has never bitten Bruno, who has trained the cat from infancy. Of course, Titus did bite...."

The ringmaster's art is brevity. The first two sentences above introduce the act and pique our interest. The rest of the introduction distracts us from Bruno's magnificence! The unneeded details dilute the power of the event.

Long, rambling meditations are usually not designed that way. **They become too long because they contain too much.** Meditations that look at more than one Scripture passage, contain more than one point, or have more than one illustration soon grow too big!

Long meditations dilute the worship experience. The minds of worshipers wander to football games, dinners, or other things. Instead of focusing attention, long meditations divert it.

5

People today are time conscious. They want to arrive at the destination on time. Traffic jams, slow drivers, and airport delays frustrate them. In worship, people know the *event* is the destination, not the meditation. Don't frustrate them by taking a scenic tour!

Remember the purpose: focus attention and attitudes on what follows. Do not use meditations to teach or preach. Stick to the point. (By all means, don't use your time in front of the microphone to talk about totally unrelated things!)

Time your meditation before giving it. Trim it to fit the time limit. When you give it, may people's attitude *not* be, "Finally! He's done!" Rather, may they anticipate the worship act.

Remember, you are not the show; you introduce it.

A New Thought Is Good

We've all watched cartoons. We know the cartoon character has a new idea when a light bulb appears over his head. When this happens the character also smiles. The cartoonist understands human nature. Seeing new insights is indeed a good experience.

One goal we have in delivering meditations is to "light the bulbs." We need to help people see new insight into the meaning of worship. If we can do this, worship will remain fresh. Several ways exist to foster new insights.

1. Use a Scripture that isn't frequently used.
2. Find a new emphasis in the passage.
3. Use an illustration that gives a new perspective.

All of these techniques are used in the example below.

Hebrews 11:4, 6 says, "By faith Abel offered God a better sacrifice than Cain did. By faith he was commended as a righteous man, when God spoke well of his offerings. And by faith he still speaks, even though he is dead. And without faith it is impossible to please God, because anyone who comes to him must believe that he exists and that he rewards those who earnestly seek him."

Kristi and Donna Jo were childhood friends. My brothers, sister, and I regularly played at their house. Then we moved away. A few years later their family traveled to visit us. The parents gave all the kids permission to eat at a pizzeria in town. Soon we were all seated around two giant pizzas. But our appetites fled when Donna Jo noticed several black, curly hairs stuck in the cheese. Something delightful and delicious had become unacceptable.

The same thing happens with God. Sometimes God finds offerings unacceptable. Hebrews reminds us that Cain and his brother Abel brought offerings to God. God accepted Abel's, but rejected Cain's. Why? This passage says the difference was the lack of faith on Cain's part. Abel was seeking a relationship with God and believed God would reward Him. Evidently Cain did not.

As you bring your offering today, what do you seek? What do you believe? Are you here to express your relationship with God? Do you believe God will reward you? I hope so. Give to God today, not just to our church. As you give, trust that God exists and will bless your life. Do this and your offering will be successful.

The Same Old Thing Is Bad

As the last strains of music fade, Susan looks toward the pulpit. "Oh no," she thinks. "Ben has the meditation. Here we go again. He's going to rant about tithing from his favorite passage." She releases a slow sigh and keeps a bland look on her face as her mind shifts away from the offering meditation. "I wonder if the Taylors have any plans after the service."

Those who give meditations on a regular basis face a danger: using the same idea over and over again. Everyone likes variety. Roast beef and mashed potatoes are good. But a steady diet of them soon brings longings for pizza!

When people repeatedly hear the same basic idea about the offering or communion, they lose focus. Like Susan above, they look at the speaker, but their minds are miles away. Even a good meditation has this effect when it becomes "the same old thing."

How can meditations be kept fresh? First, use different Scriptures. Even though a limited number of Scripture passages exist for offerings and meditations, several do exist.

Second, focus on different thoughts. Many passages contain different principles or ideas. Varying our emphasis from the passage keeps it fresh. For example, in the passage "God loves a cheerful giver," we could focus on *giver* and urge people to give (the usual emphasis). We could also emphasize *cheerful* or *loves*, talking about our attitude or God's respectively. The *Ideas* section of this book also contains several different principles to help you.

Third, use different illustrations. Since these are the most interesting part of a meditation, varying these alone can keep things fresh. Look for illustration ideas in books and magazines. Think about experiences you've had as an adult or child. Purchase communion or offering meditation books, object lesson books, or other resources. Again, the *Ideas* section of this book has several tips for illustrations.

Finally, track your meditations. Develop a system that tells you when you last used an idea. If you use a book of meditations, something as simple as writing the date on the page when you use an idea helps. If you write your own meditations, also jot the date you used it on the back of the paper or index card.

STORIES ARE GOOD

John Maxwell teaches about tithing by telling the following story:

A father decided to buy his son some french fries at the local fast food restaurant. No special occasion, he just wanted to take his son out for a special treat. After ordering the fries and sitting in the booth, the father reached across the table to take a few fries.

"Mine!" the boy said, as he pushed the fries away from his father.

The father was hurt. Why? He certainly didn't need the fries. He could buy all the fries he wanted. He could have bought enough fries to bury his son! He was hurt because his son lacked gratitude. After all, the father bought the fries and only wanted a small portion in return.

Imagine how God sees us. He is the source of blessing in our lives. He gives us so much. When we refuse to return a tithe to Him, it displays immaturity and a lack of gratitude. God doesn't need our money. We need to honor God with our money.

Stories and illustrations like this one are very effective in meditations. First, they capture attention. Everyone loves a good story. Stories perk up the audience's attention level. Imagine how effective this story would capture attention if it were introduced by holding up an empty french fry carton from the restaurant!

Second, stories help us connect emotionally. Most of us know how the dad in this story felt. We experience a little of his emotion as the story is told. Then, while identifying with the story, the connection is made to tithing. We understand how our refusal to tithe displays a shameful lack of gratitude to God.

Third, stories "fly in under the radar." People may have a resistant attitude to the offering. They may mentally brace themselves against persuasion from the speaker. A good story acts like a military jet avoiding radar to get close to the target. It avoids their resistance and gets closer to their hearts.

Stories can be found in many places, such as personal experience, newspapers and magazines, and in illustration books or databases. Always watch for a good story that can be used in a meditation. Try to include one in every meditation.

Boring Is Bad

One of the most boring things I've ever read was an assignment in college. It covered several hundred pages. The author wrote in long, complex sentences. His paragraphs stretched for several lines. Absolutely nothing of interest broke the monotonous words—no humor, stories, or application to modern life. The more I read, the sleepier I got. Night after night I stared at the pages until the words seemed to swim before my eyes. The only reason I read was to receive class credit. To this day, I can't remember a thing from the book.

People can force themselves to pay attention to boring things, but it takes effort. They only do it when required by something like a work or school assignment. Even when they "have to" focus on boring material, they don't "want to."

A boring meditation is a waste of time for the speaker and the audience. Thankfully, the formula for a good meditation is easy: use one Scripture and one story to make one point. The danger of being boring comes when an element is lacking or too many elements are added.

Compare the following meditation fragments. They are about the same length, but one is far more interesting.

Example 1: "Luke 21:1–4 teaches us that Jesus pays attention to the percentage of income we give. He praised the widow because she gave so much. Two copper coins were small compared to what the rich people gave. They gave large amounts! But compared to what she kept for herself, the widow's coins were huge. As you give your offering today, consider the percentage. Jesus cares less about the dollar amount, and more about the percentage amount of your offering. How big is your gift anyway? Some here will give many dollars, others only a few. Remember, the true size of your gift is the percentage of your income it represents.

Example 2: "Have you noticed the old woman who sits downtown by Minuteman Press? She's not a bag lady, but you know she's poor. Her clothes are old. She usually wears an old tattered scarf. She walks with pain. Look the next time you're on Columbia Street. She's usually sitting on the bench, often sipping a soda or coffee. When I read Luke 21:1–4, I picture a woman like this, hardly noticed, placing her coins in the box. The widow impressed Jesus, not on the dollar amount of her offering, but on the percentage amount she gave. Look at your offering today through the eyes of Jesus.

Spice up your meditations with stories, visual descriptions, and object lessons. Do this, and people with look forward to your words.

HUMOR IS GOOD

Nothing relaxes tension as well as humor. I was attending a large meeting. As the speaker began the offering meditation, he asked us to stand. He then told us to reach into the pocket of the person in front of us and take out the wallet and give generously! The crowd chuckled heartily! He then explained how easy it was to give away money that doesn't belong to you. He concluded by reading a Scripture that showed everything really belongs to God.

You have probably experienced this stunt, too. It became very popular. Why did it work? Because it made people laugh. Offering time can be a tense time. People may be uncomfortable because they know they should give or give more than they do. They may also be expecting someone to manipulate them with guilt. Humor relieves this tension.

Humor can also tell the truth in a less painful way. Consider the following example of a humorous meditation. It is rather pointed, but it relieves the tension with a joke.

Four-year-old Mary was quite pleased to receive a dollar on her birthday. She carried the bill about the house and was seen sitting on the stairs admiring it.

"What are you going to do with your dollar?" her mother asked.

"Take it to Sunday School," said Mary promptly.

"To show your teacher?"

Mary shook her head. "No," she said. "I'm going to give it to God. He'll be as surprised as I am to get something besides pennies."

You know, some people are like Mary's Sunday School classmates. They give an offering to God, but of a token amount, never realizing that a token offering can insult God. Would a good waitress who served several people a large meal be pleased with spare change for a tip, or insulted? This explains God's sense of injustice in Malachi 3:8–10: "Will a man rob God? Yet you rob me. But you ask, 'How do we rob you?' In tithes and offerings. You are under a curse—the whole nation of you—because you are robbing me. Bring the *whole* tithe into the storehouse, that there may be food in my house."

Some Christians are more dedicated to tipping good waitresses than to tithing to our awesome God. Come on! Be like Mary and surprise someone! Why not offer more than a token amount to God today?!

GUILT IS BAD

Fred looked sternly at the congregation. He read Malachi 3:8–10 in serious tones. He fixed the audience with a stare and began his comments. "Some of you in this church are thieves! You do not tithe! When you don't tithe, you rob God! Shame on you!" He continued for a couple of minutes exhorting people to tithe. When the offering was gathered, it contained the usual amount.

Many well-intentioned people like Fred exist. They mistakenly think Scripture reads, "God loves a *squirming* giver"! They have an honest desire to help people honor God with the offering. Usually, however, this approach does not motivate people to give. God has a better way.

Scripture says God loves the *cheerful* giver. This makes sense. Every merchant worth his salt knows people spend more money when in a positive, cheerful mood. They train their staff and arrange the environment to put people at ease. Their sales force is told to smile and be cheerful. Think about it: would you buy a car from a salesman who made you feel guilty? Probably not.

Not only does cheerfulness work, it honors God. God's desire is not just to receive money, He wants to receive the attitude of joy and love. We have not performed our job if people simply give out of sullen or shamefaced duty.

Meditations usually should not manipulate people's guilt. Our goal should be producing an attitude of cheerfulness, not guilt. Present the joys of giving and let the Holy Spirit deal with people's hearts.

A good friend of mine says "sugar your gums" before speaking to another on a sensitive topic. Consider the following comments, again based on Malachi 3:8–10. Rather than producing guilt, they focus on the guilt-free feeling of tithing.

Have you ever thought about how it feels to be a thief? Thieves are always hiding, looking over their shoulder, anxious about being caught. They feel guilty. They certainly don't have joy. I don't want you to feel that way!

You live honest and upright lives. You enjoy life because you're not worried about being caught. A similar joy is found by those who tithe. They can relax and enjoy God even more, because they treat God with the honor He deserves. Think about how good it feels to tithe! Think how comfortable the offering becomes! If you don't tithe, try it! You'll like how it feels!

Practical Matters

DELIVERING MEDITATIONS

What would life be without the remote control? How we love the ease and control it offers us. Let's face it: channel surfing is fast becoming the American pasttime! Even before owning a television with a remote control, I used to lie in the floor to watch, using my big toe to change channels!

Remote control allows us to quickly switch away from objectionable material, check the scores on the other game, surf during commercials, or search for something interesting to watch. Imagine the challenge to advertisers and programmers. If a viewer's attention isn't captured within seconds, he or she moves on. In addition, any time the viewer becomes bored the channel is changed.

People also do this mentally. Their minds can change channels instantly during the worship service. Our challenge in delivering meditations is to capture attention within seconds, hold it, and direct it to the offering or communion. The content of our meditation is crucial to this goal. But so is our delivery. Here are several tips on delivering meditations to keep the "channel surfers" on target.

1. Acquaint yourself with the pulpit, microphone and microphone switch before the service. Know the "on" position for the switch in case you need to change it.
2. Keep the "flow"of the service going. If a song precedes the meditation, move into position before it ends. Begin the medi-

tation *immediately* after the music (or preceding element). Stop those "surfers"!

3. Smile and look at the people. Smile again! If you are nervous looking directly at the faces of people, look directly over the heads of those on the back row.

4. Talk toward the microphone, not down at the pulpit or notes. You may need to hold your Bible or notes chest high in order to speak toward the microphone and maintain eye contact with the audience. If you are not using a microphone, talk loudly enough to be heard on the back row.

5. Do not read the meditation. Memorize the opening sentence or two and deliver them looking at the people. Highlight the major points in the meditation. Try to keep your eyes up, glancing at your notes as needed.

6. Finish strong. Don't be like an airplane circling the airport and never landing. Know the last sentence you will speak before you begin. This will help you end well.

Writing Meditations

How powerful I felt carrying Grandpa's old shotgun! Dad, my brother Roger, and I had been pheasant hunting that cold Kansas morning, when Dad spotted ducks on the pond. We circled into position. The north wind cut into our faces as we walked slowly up the draw toward the pond.

We climbed the dam. Dozens of mallards jumped into the air. I picked a duck, aimed and felt the gun smack my shoulder as the duck dropped. Other shots rang out. The ducks caught the wind, veered over our heads and disappeared. Well, all the ducks except the two lying on the water.

Dad grinned, "We got 'em!" We gathered to compare notes. Three hunters and two ducks. Somebody had missed and the look on Roger's face said it all. As we talked Dad recognized the problem and gently explained, "You can't shoot at the whole flock! Pick one duck and aim at it." Dad gave his duck to Roger and we all strutted home.

Writing good meditations is the same as shooting ducks. Take aim, don't shoot at everything! **Use *one* Scripture and *one* illustration to make *one* point.** Ecclesiastes 6:11 says, "The more the words, the less the meaning, and how does that profit anyone?"

The words above are an example of a good meditation, although it is a meditation about meditations! In writing it, I aimed to make one point—the statement in bold type. I used a story to focus attention and show the importance of good aim. This principle was also taught by the Scripture.

I also stripped the story of excess information, leaving just enough to make it interesting. I didn't mention the type of guns we carried, how we were dressed, ages, where the pond was in relation to the house, our preparation for the hunt, etc. Some of that information I find fascinating, such as Dad using baling wire to hang the ducks from the hammer-loops of our insulated coveralls! But including this information would detract from the main point about good aim.

To write a good meditation, do the following:

1. Write the point you want to make in one short sentence. Try to use a dozen words or less. This point may be the words of a Scripture passage, such as "God loves a cheerful giver," or "the tithe belongs to God."

2. Select an illustration that is interesting and supports your aim.

3. Organize and trim your words.

4. Adjust and rewrite it until it focuses attention and sets the attitude.

CUSTOMIZING MEDITATIONS

Writing a meditation often takes more time that we have. Often we find meditations in books or magazines. How can we use these effectively? Customize them. Customizing makes them more interesting. A sample illustration follows the three steps to customize a meditation. Each step also contains instructions in parentheses to practice on the sample which follows.

1. *Analyze the meditation.* What point does it try to make? Is it the right length? Remember the formula: use one Scripture and one main illustration to make one point. Does it make too many points? Does it use too many Scriptures? Do the illustrations match your audience? Farm illustrations may be lost on an urban congregation, and vice versa. (In the sample below, circle the words that seem to be the main point. Will this meditation work for your audience?)

2. *Personalize the meditation.* Can you substitute or add illustrations from your own life that make the point? Do the words of the meditation match the words you use? Can you adapt the language to sound more like you? Remember, never read meditations. Tell them in your own words. (Think of the most cheerful person you know. Substitute a story about that person for the story about John Thybault. Pick a story that contrasts

cheerfulness with whining or complaining. Write the person's name and a few facts about the story in the margin. Try *telling* your customized meditation without reading it.)

3. *Familiarize yourself with the meditation.* Writing meditations naturally makes them familiar. Using meditations written by another requires effort to learn them. Read it several times. Try saying it aloud in your own words. (Practice giving your customized meditation a few times. Time it and adjust it to make the main point.)

2 Corinthians 9:7 says, "Each man should give what he has decided in his heart to give, not reluctantly or under compulsion, for God loves a cheerful giver."

One of the most cheerful people I know is John Thybault. John and his wife lived across the hall in our college apartment building. I loved to talk to John! He always smiled and seemed happy to see me. He had enthusiasm for life.

Several times John and his wife baby sat an infant with colic. The poor child never seemed happy. It cried constantly. We could hear the crying in our apartment. Nobody likes to hear babies cry. We'd rather hear them laugh.

As you give your offering today, what should your attitude be? Don't be a crybaby. Don't give reluctantly. As you place your gift into the offering, smile! Bring cheerfulness to God, not just your money. God loves a cheerful giver.

Ready-To-Use Offering Meditations

THE OFFERING IS IMPORTANT

Do you remember going to school? The teacher was always telling us things, wasn't she? Some of the things were important for reading or math. Others were instructions on how to line up for lunch or recess. She told us of tornado and fire drills and of take-home papers.

As a child, how did we know which of these things were more important? We knew because she told us the important things early and often. Consider Genesis 4:3, "In the course of time Cain brought some of the fruits of the soil as an offering to the Lord."

This is the first usage of the word *offering* in the Bible. In fact, this is the first worship of God mentioned after the Garden of Eden. This worship centered on presenting an offering to God.

This was the first use of the word, but certainly not the last. In the New International Version the word *offering* is used 675 times. Just how important is this concept?

Well, consider these facts:

- The word *love* is used over a hundred times less than the word *offering*.
- *Offering* is used about twice as often as the word *praise* and more than twice as often as the word *faith*.

Since the word *offering* is given early and often, we can conclude that it is very important! It is not as important as the word *God* (used

3979 times) or the word *Jesus* (used 1275 times). But it is certainly very important.

Today, center your heart in worship to God as you present your offering. This act is far more important that we normally think.

YOUR OFFERING IS EVIDENCE OF YOUR HEART

Police rope off the scene of a crime. They photograph, measure, take samples and fingerprints, and interview witnesses and neighbors. They are looking for evidence. Sometimes the evidence is as small as a fiber, hair, or the blood type of a sample. At other times it is as large as footprints or tire tracks.

The evidence will point them to the perpetrator. Even if the crime was not witnessed, some types of evidence will still convict. The same evidence will also clear others of the crime. The list of suspects will be narrowed because the evidence points to their innocence.

In Genesis 4:3–4 the offerings of Cain and Abel are evidence of their heart. "In the course of time Cain brought some of the fruits of the soil as an offering to the LORD. But Abel brought fat portions from some of the firstborn of his flock. The LORD looked with favor on Abel and his offering, but on Cain and his offering he did not look with favor. So Cain was very angry, and his face was downcast."

We are told in Hebrews 11 that the difference between the two was the faith in Abel's heart. God accepted his offering. Cain's anger resulted from a heart that was already wrong before God.

Remember, as you present your offering today it is evidence of your heart. What you give and the amount you give are important. But God is most concerned with the attitude in which you give it. Approach God with faith, humility and love.

Honor God With Your Offering

Have you ever seen a soldier or sailor with a chest full of ribbons and medals? Our country honors soldiers in this way. The greatest of these medals is the Congressional Medal of Honor. This medal is only awarded to deserving men or women who risked their lives far above and beyond the call of duty. Most who have received it were seriously injured or killed in the action.

Soldiers are honored for what they do. We honor God for what he has done as well as for who he is. He is the great Creator and Ruler of the world. He is the Savior. He deserves far more honor than a medal from Congress.

So how can we show this honor to God? He doesn't have a uniform upon which to pin a medal. Ribbons or trophies are not of much use either. Notice how Jacob honored God in Genesis 35:9–15.

> After Jacob returned from Paddan Aram, God appeared to him again and blessed him. God said to him, "Your name is Jacob, but you will no longer be called Jacob; your name will be Israel." So he named him Israel. And God said to him, "I am God Almighty; be fruitful and increase in number. A nation and a community of nations will come from you, and kings will come from your body. The land I gave to Abraham and Isaac I also give to you, and I will give this

land to your descendants after you." Then God went up from him at the place where he had talked with him. Jacob set up a stone pillar at the place where God had talked with him, and he poured out a drink offering on it; he also poured oil on it.

Jacob did two things. First, set up a monument. Then he poured an offering of wine on the monument.

Today, we bring our offerings to God. This money is a small token of the honor he deserves as our Savior and Lord. Let us now present our offerings to honor our God.

TRUST GOD TO PROVIDE

The primitive tribesmen of Australia use a hunting club with a highly effective aerodynamic design. We call it the boomerang. Thrown properly, it lifts into a high sweeping curve and returns to the thrower. You can trust wind and aerodynamic laws to return it each time.

You can also trust God to return what is given. Hebrews 11:17–19 says, "By faith Abraham, when God tested him, offered Isaac as a sacrifice. He who had received the promises was about to sacrifice his one and only son, even though God had said to him, 'It is through Isaac that your offspring will be reckoned.' Abraham reasoned that God could raise the dead, and figuratively speaking, he did receive Isaac back from death."

We marvel at Abraham's faith! He was willing to kill and burn his son on an altar as a sacrifice to God. Yet Abraham's faith made perfect sense to him. He looked past the gift and saw the power of God to return the promised son from the dead.

We may marvel at Abraham's faith, but I wonder if he would marvel at our lack of it. We place our trust in the aerodynamic principles that make boomerangs and airplanes fly, but hesitate when given the opportunity to place faith in God.

God promises to supply your needs if you honor him with an offering today. He promises to bless you generously for your generosity. Look past the gift and see the power of God to return it. Express your faith in God by giving generously today.

SHOW YOUR THANKFULNESS

"Count off seven weeks from the time you begin to put the sickle to the standing grain. Then celebrate the Feast of Weeks to the LORD your God by giving a freewill offering in proportion to the blessings the LORD your God has given you." Deuteronomy 16:9–10

The Feast of Weeks was similar to our Thanksgiving holiday. It celebrated a good harvest and the blessings of God. Work halted for the holiday. Religious services were held.

But the Feast of Weeks was different from Thanksgiving. The primary focus of Thanksgiving is a family dinner of turkey and pumpkin pie. The primary focus of the Feast of Weeks was an offering given to God.

This offering was proportional. If you had a big harvest, you gave a big offering. If you had a small harvest, you gave a small offering. In fact, Deuteronomy 16:16–17 says, "No man should appear before the LORD empty-handed: Each of you must bring a gift in proportion to the way the LORD your God has blessed you."

Today, we gather to worship our Lord and God. Show your thankfulness to God with your offering. Let your offering be proportional to your income. If God has blessed you richly, give a rich offering. If you have not been blessed, give accordingly. The easiest way to give proportionally is to give ten percent of your income.

Remember, show your thankfulness by giving an offering to God.

OFFER THE PROPER THINGS

"Aaron's sons Nadab and Abihu took their censers, put fire in them and added incense; and they offered unauthorized fire before the LORD, contrary to his command. So fire came out from the presence of the LORD and consumed them, and they died before the LORD." Leviticus 10:1–2

Imagine how shocked people were when fire consumed these priests during the worship service! Wouldn't you be shocked if fire leaped from the offering plate and killed someone today? If it happened just once, we'd be passing that plate like a hot potato! We'd all be alert at offering time, wouldn't we?

What was the problem with Nadab and Abihu's offering of incense? The Bible says it was contrary to God's command. It violated the techniques that God commanded them to observe. By breaking the rules, Nadab and Abihu showed contempt for God.

I'm thankful that we do not have the same rules governing our offerings. God grants us great freedom. We are free to decide the amount of our offering. We are also free to vary our particular offering ceremony.

Although the rules for the offering have changed since Nadab and Abihu's time, God has not. He is the same awesome being who demands and deserves respect. The offering is just as important as the communion, prayer, the sermon, or any other part of our worship. It is a way we express honor, faith and love for our Creator and Savior.

As in the time of Nadab and Abihu, we must offer to God the proper things. Be sure you give more than money today. Show your respect. Show your submission to God through this offering.

Experiencing God Motivates Our Giving

Ride a roller coaster and you experience thrills, a bit of fear, and a little dizziness. The bigger the roller coaster, the more powerful the sensations and the more people love them. Modern coasters loop and twist through a steel maze. Designers are constantly dreaming up new rides to create new thrills. Theme parks invest millions of dollars in roller coasters because they attract more customers to the park than any other ride. When a new roller coaster opens, attendance at the park soars.

A roller coaster ride is a powerful experience. More powerful is experiencing God. One day Gideon was out working on his grain harvest when the angel of the Lord appeared to him. Notice how Gideon was motivated by his divine experience in Judges 6:17–18, "Gideon replied, 'If now I have found favor in your eyes, give me a sign that it is really you talking to me. Please do not go away until I come back and bring my offering and set it before you.' And the LORD said, 'I will wait until you return.'"

If you know the story, you know that God wanted Gideon to lead his people to defeat the oppressing Midianites. This event obviously helped motivate Gideon to rally the troops and defeat the enemy. But it was not Gideon's first reaction. His first reaction was to present an offering to God.

Experiencing God in our lives is a powerful motivation. Remember your salvation experience? Remember some of the special answers to prayer you have received? Have you experienced times when you felt God's presence in a special way? Each of these should motivate us to live holy lives. I think they should also motivate us to present an offering to God.

The thrill of the roller coaster draws people to the theme park. It draw the riders from one coaster to the next. Some simply exit the ride and immediately get back in line. God's salvation and power thrill us. They motivates us to give. They draw us to worship because we want to experience more of God.

WHO DESERVES MONEY?

Parents teach important lessons about money to their children. "Money doesn't grow on trees." "You get what you pay for." "Keep it from burning a hole in your pocket." These are all common sayings about money. But perhaps one of the most repeated lessons about money are these three words: "Get a job."

We all learn that the way to acquire wealth is to earn it. Children and teens often want something. They also want their parents to buy it. Children who are spoiled, and get everything they want, develop an attitude of entitlement. They think the world owes them. They want everything "handed to them on a silver platter."

But no human being deserves wealth simply because he or she exists. We resent this attitude in others. Perhaps that's why we struggle to give offerings to God. God *expects* an offering from us. He wants us to bring money to him. He seems to think he is entitled. Who does he think he is? Oh yeah, he *is* God.

Psalm 96:8 says, "Ascribe to the LORD the glory due his name; bring an offering and come into his courts." Praise and offerings are God's due. He deserves it simply because he is God. He also deserves it for the things he has done.

When your children come to you with their hands out, the best thing to say may be, "Get a job." But we need a different attitude when we come to God. He expects an offering. We should bring one and say, "O Lord, you deserve this and more."

PLEASING TO GOD

"I have received full payment and even more; I am amply supplied, now that I have received from Epaphroditus the gifts you sent. They are a fragrant offering, an acceptable sacrifice, pleasing to God." Philippians 4:18

Have you ever given a gift and then wondered if the person really liked it? Maybe it was a gift to a girlfriend or boyfriend, or perhaps a gift to your spouse. As he or she opened it you watched for a reaction. You may have asked, "Do you like it?"

Gifts are given to please others. When the person is really special to you, you yearn to please them. I know that God has a special place in your heart. I know you long to please him. Perhaps you wonder if he really likes the gift you brought today. Be assured that he does!

In this passage Paul says their gift was pleasing to God. He also calls it "fragrant." Can't you imagine someone taking a deep breath of a pleasant aroma and saying, "Mmmmm"? Keep this picture in your mind today. As you give your gift, realize that it pleases God.

SHOW HONOR TO GOD

I'm sure you've seen the Academy Awards on television. To honor the best talent in film golden statues are presented amidst loud applause. The winner is made the center of attention. In the awards program for music or television, the format is the same. The only change is in the gift given to the winners. We often honor people by giving a gift.

Daniel was a great prophet of God. His king, Nebuchadnezzar, was troubled by a dream. The king wanted his dream explained. Not only that, he wanted someone to retell the dream without being told about it. If none of his advisors could retell the dream and explain it, they would all be killed. The only one able to do both tasks was Daniel. Daniel 2:46 tells what the king did when Daniel explained his dream, "Then King Nebuchadnezzar fell prostrate before Daniel and paid him honor and ordered that an offering and incense be presented to him."

The king showed great honor to Daniel. He made him the center of attention and gave him an offering. He also placed burning incense before him. Nebuchadnezzar actually showed honor to God by honoring God's prophet Daniel.

We have come here today to honor our God. He knows our deeds. He even knows our dreams. He deserves our worship and praise. We make him the center of attention and bring offerings. Honor God with your offering now.

Show Your Eagerness to Help

Some children are eager to help. When dad pops open the hood of the car, they want to climb up and help. When mom mixes up a cake or cookies, they want to stir the batter. If a repair man comes to fix an appliance, they try to squat down near him and get involved.

We see this eagerness to help in the children's actions. Their faces shows it. Words also show it as they beg, "Mommy, please!"

One reason we give our offerings is an eagerness to help. In 2 Corinthians 8:19 Paul talks about the offerings that the churches were collecting to help with famine relief. He explained that the offering was being collected to "honor the Lord himself and to show our eagerness to help."

This offering is a way you can help. You help meet the expenses of our congregation. You help provide teaching for our people. But more importantly, you help in the work of the kingdom of God. Your offering helps us do God's work of making disciples and sharing God's love.

Can you be like a little child today? Show your eagerness to help. May it show in your face. May it show in your words. May it show in your actions as you give generously to honor our Lord and to help his church.

LET YOUR GRATITUDE FLOW

The classic martial arts demonstration is breaking a board with one karate chop. We've seen it on television dozens of times. We've seen the variations of using the foot or elbow or head. We've probably seen dozens of boards broken at once, or concrete blocks, or some other amazing feat.

The experts tell us the secret to these feats of strength is channeling all of the energy of the blow into one small area. The power and force of the legs and torso must flow through the punch. Proper footwork and technique are studied and practiced to accomplish this.

What do karate chops have to do with the offering? More than you might imagine. The connection is the idea of letting energy flow through one small area. For the offering, that energy is a sense of gratitude.

Psalm 54:6–7 says, "I will sacrifice a freewill offering to you; I will praise your name, O LORD, for it is good. For he has delivered me from all my troubles, and my eyes have looked in triumph on my foes."

The psalmist's gratitude for God's deliverance flowed forth in an offering. This was not a required offering; it was given freely. You will also give freely when you let your gratitude flow. Learn the secret of martial arts. Focus the flow of your gratitude to God through one small area—your wallet!

Ready-To-Use
Communion Meditations

FAMILY TRADITIONS

Families develop traditions. Does your family have a tradition about where it eats Thanksgiving dinner? Do you have traditions about Christmas decorations or when the presents are opened? Does your family have a reunion they traditionally hold each summer? Every family has some traditions.

God's family also has traditions. In ancient Israel one of the traditions was called Passover. Each year, each family gathered to kill and roast a lamb. This tradition is rooted in God's deliverance of the ancient Israelites from slavery. Exodus 12:21–23 tells about the original observance:

> Then Moses summoned all the elders of Israel and said to them, "Go at once and select the animals for your families and slaughter the Passover lamb. Take a bunch of hyssop, dip it into the blood in the basin and put some of the blood on the top and on both sides of the door frame. Not one of you shall go out the door of his house until morning. When the LORD goes through the land to strike down the Egyptians, he will see the blood on the top and sides of the door frame and will pass over that doorway, and he will not permit the destroyer to enter your houses and strike you down."

The annual tradition of eating a Passover meal reminded the Israelites of God's deliverance from slavery in Egypt. We are God's family today. We also have a tradition. The Lord's Supper reminds us of God's deliverance from sin. Jesus' blood, like that of the Passover lamb, protects us from God's judgment upon sin. This observance reminds us of the blood Jesus shed for us.

THE BURDEN OF CARE

"He was despised and rejected by men, a man of sorrows, and familiar with suffering. Like one from whom men hide their faces he was despised, and we esteemed him not. Surely he took up our infirmities and carried our sorrows, yet we considered him stricken by God, smitten by him, and afflicted. But he was pierced for our transgressions, he was crushed for our iniquities; the punishment that brought us peace was upon him, and by his wounds we are healed" Isaiah 53:3–5.

Have you ever considered how important nurses are to health? They are the unsung heros of health care. Doctors order the care for patients, but nurses deliver it. They quietly carry the burden of care. Although they dispense medication, kind words and comfort, much of their job is distasteful. They change blood-soaked dressings, stick people with needles, and carry away bodily fluids and filth. Yet the patient's recovery depends on their care.

Jesus is the hero of salvation. This we know. But consider how distasteful his sacrifice was. He was burdened with our care and healing. He carried away our spiritual filth.

But Jesus' efforts were not simply carrying the burden of our care. He gave his life that we may be healed. Although nurses are noble and kind, they do not shed their blood for a dying patient. They don't give their lives so the patient might live. But Jesus did. That's why we remember and honor him with this observance.

THE BOND OF LOVE

The bond of affection between a pet and its owner can be very strong. If you own a cat or dog, you understand this. If you return home after a long absence, your pet is excited to see you. A pet owner often spends lots of time and money caring for the animal. A shepherd has a similar level of care for his sheep.

John 10:14–15 says, "I am the good shepherd; I know my sheep and my sheep know me—just as the Father knows me and I know the Father—and I lay down my life for the sheep."

A shepherd knows the sheep much like a pet owner knows the pet. If a wolf threatens the flock, the shepherd risks his life to save the sheep. Most pet owners would also rush to rescue their animals from a similar threat.

Jesus loves us as a shepherd loves his sheep. Our Good Shepherd, however, didn't simply risk his life. He knowingly sacrificed it. He willingly submitted to death on the cross. This is the love and care we remember with this simple ceremony of bread and the fruit of the vine. They remind us that Jesus knows us. But the bread, representing his body, and the cup, representing his shed blood, remind us that Jesus' love is greater than any—he gave his life for us.

Any Volunteers?

Would anyone here like to be diagnosed with cancer? Surely not. We dread the disease. Many of us have seen the devastation it brings. We've seen the sickness and suffering. We've probably known someone who died of cancer.

Would you volunteer to be infected with terminal cancer? Would you be infected if it would cure your neighbor down the street? Would you be infected to end world hunger? What would it take to make you volunteer to die of cancer?

We don't like thinking about this, do we? I can hardly imagine any reason you or I would volunteer for death by cancer. Why would we exchange good health for suffering and death? Yet Jesus volunteered for something similar. He volunteered for death by sin.

2 Corinthians 5:21 says, "God made him who had no sin to be sin for us, so that in him we might become the righteousness of God."

In a spiritual sense sin is like cancer. It devastates and destroys. It causes suffering and death. Jesus was willing to experience that suffering and death in our place. He was perfectly holy. He had never sinned. Yet he volunteered to experience the suffering and death that sin brings. What made him do it? He loved you. He did it so you could be cured. He died so you and I could become righteous in him. As you partake today, remember that Jesus volunteered to die for you.

A REAL CURSE

"All who rely on observing the law are under a curse, for it is written: 'Cursed is everyone who does not continue to do everything written in the Book of the Law'" Galatians 3:10.

What does the word *curse* bring to your mind? Do you think of the old Disney movie about a man who became a shaggy dog because of the curse on some old ring? Do you think about the stories of *Sleeping Beauty* or of *Beauty and the Beast*? To us, curses are the things of fantasy and fairy tales. They are entertaining plot devices, but hardly something we confront every day.

This verse is not a fairy tale. It speaks of a very real curse. Everyone who bases his or her relationship to God on living a good life is cursed. We are not cursed because we want to live a good life. The curse comes because we don't live a *perfectly* good life. This curse is the condemnation we face for breaking God's laws.

Jesus provides release from this curse. Galatians 3:13 says, "Christ redeemed us from the curse of the law by becoming a curse for us, for it is written: 'Cursed is everyone who is hung on a tree.'" Through his crucifixion Jesus assumed the curse. He paid the price. He endured the condemnation for us. We now base our relationship with God on faith in Jesus, not in trusting our own goodness.

The Lord's Supper reminds us of a true story. It is the story about a curse upon us which was removed when Jesus became cursed for us.

A Terrible Price

Have you been shocked at the price of something? Have you experienced "sticker shock" when shopping for a car? Maybe you have been shocked by the cost of health care or auto repair. You simply can't believe the price is so high. Leviticus also gives us sticker shock over the price of forgiveness.

Leviticus 4:27–31 says:

> If a member of the community sins unintentionally and does what is forbidden in any of the Lord's commands, he is guilty. When he is made aware of the sin he committed, he must bring as his offering for the sin he committed a female goat without defect. He is to lay his hand on the head of the sin offering and slaughter it at the place of the burnt offering. Then the priest is to take some of the blood with his finger and put it on the horns of the altar of burnt offering and pour out the rest of the blood at the base of the altar. He shall remove all the fat, just as the fat is removed from the fellowship offering, and the priest shall burn it on the altar as an aroma pleasing to the LORD. In this way the priest will make atonement for him, and he will be forgiven.

I'm glad I didn't live in the ancient nation of Israel! Can you imagine having to kill a goat every time you sin?! I would have run out of goats a long time ago! Most of you would have run out too!

Forgiveness of sin comes at a terrible price. It requires death. The ancient Israelites learned about this price through the slaughter of their livestock. Imagine the emotional impact of seeing a living animal killed, bled, and burned in a few short minutes.

The Bible tells us the ancient system of sacrifice wasn't ultimately effective. It simply awaited the perfect sacrifice of God's Son. Yet we see the same lesson in each, namely, forgiveness of sin comes at a terrible price. The bread and cup of communion remind us of the body and blood of Jesus. The death of Jesus is the terrible price of our forgiveness.

YOUR SIN IS COVERED

Do you remember getting a skinned elbow or knee as a child? Maybe you wrecked your bike or skates. Perhaps you got a grass burn playing ball. However it happened, you felt stinging pain and looked down to see a large, raw area of missing skin.

Wow, did that thing hurt! Washing it with water hurt! Even when the wound was clean, the breeze blowing across it hurt! Remember how soothing it was to have the scrape covered with ointment and a large bandage? It still stung a little, but it always felt better to have it covered, especially after the invention of the "ouchless" bandage.

Our sin also wounds us. Our emotions sting with the guilt over our past. I'm sure you've felt this pain too. Sometimes it seems like the pain of guilt will never go away.

The Lord's Supper relieves this pain. It reminds us of our forgiveness through Jesus' death. Like an "ouchless" bandage, his death covered our sins. It provides the healing we need while the Supper soothes and reassures us. Although our sin may still sting a little, the pain of guilt is gone.

Psalm 32:1–2 says, "Blessed is he whose transgressions are forgiven, whose sins are covered. Blessed is the man whose sin the LORD does not count against him and in whose spirit is no deceit."

Today, as you partake of communion, say to yourself, "My sins are covered." Focus upon the forgiveness accomplished for you by Jesus. Let this be a soothing time of spiritual healing and reassurance.

SHOW ME

"Show me." Have you ever uttered those words? Missouri may be known as the Show Me State, but everyone has a bit of this attitude.

One child bragging about his abilities is challenged by another with, "Prove it."

An adolescent athlete urges the coach to let him onto the team. "Show me what you can do," the coach replies.

At a job application an employer seeks a demonstration of skill from the applicant. Before taking a risk with a new employee, he wants to know the person can do the job.

Even in the NBA finals, one player often challenges his opponent to prove he is a winner. The superstar responds by lifting the team to victory with scoring and teamwork.

Have you ever wanted to say to God, "Prove it"? You really don't need to, because God has already demonstrated his ability. He has proved his love, grace, and justice. Listen to Romans 3:23–26, "for all have sinned and fall short of the glory of God, and are justified freely by his grace through the redemption that came by Christ Jesus. God presented him as a sacrifice of atonement, through faith in his blood. He did this to demonstrate his justice, because in his forbearance he had left the sins committed beforehand unpunished—he did it to demonstrate his justice at the present time, so as to be just and the one who justifies those who have faith in Jesus."

The death of Christ proved God's love, grace and justice. The Lord's Supper reminds us. Like the scoreboard lit long after the game, it declares the contest won. In this observance today, thank God for proving his grace and justice through Jesus' death.

CLEANSED FOR A PURPOSE

Do you remember preparing for your high school prom? We showered and scrubbed. We splashed on cologne or perfume. We donned clean, pressed dresses or tuxedos. Unless we rented a limo, the men probably vacuumed, washed, and polished the car. We literally spent hours cleaning and preparing ourselves for the special night.

The Lord's Supper reminds us of a spiritual cleansing. Through the death of Christ our sins were cleansed. Hebrews 9:14 says, "How much more, then, will the blood of Christ, who through the eternal Spirit offered himself unblemished to God, cleanse our consciences from acts that lead to death, so that we may serve the living God!"

We often focus on our cleansing from sin in the communion service. We rightly remember the total forgiveness Jesus accomplished for us. We celebrate our freedom from guilt. Today, however, I want us to focus on the purpose of our cleansing. Listen again to this phrase from the passage, "so that we may serve the living God!"

In high school, we cleansed ourselves for a special purpose: the prom. Jesus also cleansed us for a special purpose: to serve God. As you partake of the communion today, remember the purpose of your cleansing from sin. Examine your life and how well you have been serving the living God. Pray silently and express your submission to Jesus as Lord.

ONCE FOR ALL

I'm sure everyone here has received a tetanus vaccination. You probably experienced the bruising and soreness in your arm for a few days. Although the vaccination protects from disease, I'm sure you didn't enjoy it.

The problem with tetanus vaccinations is their length of effectiveness. They only last a certain number of years. Then we have to take another one of those shots! We have to experience the soreness and pain all over again. No one looks forward to a tetanus booster! Don't you wish someone would invent a one-time tetanus vaccine?

Thankfully, we have a one-time cure for our sin. Jesus' death never loses its effectiveness. As Hebrews 10:10 says, "And by that will, we have been made holy through the sacrifice of the body of Jesus Christ once for all."

What does it mean to be made holy? It means we have been set apart and made special to God. It means we have been made acceptable to God. It means God has cleansed our sin through the sacrifice of Christ.

The Lord's Supper is not a spiritual booster shot. We don't need it because the death of Jesus has lost effectiveness for us. We observe it as those who have been made holy, "once for all." It reminds us of the tremendous power of Christ's death to make us holy to God.

SEND YOUR LOVE

Greeting card companies make a good business by providing ways for people to send their love. We may send cards to someone grieving. At other times we send a greeting to congratulate someone on an accomplishment. A great number of cards are sent to express romance and commitment between spouses or between dating couples. For every expression of love and caring, a card exists.

Greeting card companies also compete for business. One company uses the slogan "when you care enough to send the very best." Others specialize in a particular style of humor or greeting. Some styles are poetic and glamorous. Others are modern or quirky.

When God wanted to send his very best, he did not send a card. He sent his Son. As 1 John 4:9–10 says, "This is how God showed his love among us: He sent his one and only Son into the world that we might live through him. This is love: not that we loved God, but that he loved us and sent his Son as an atoning sacrifice for our sins."

No one can compete with this love. No company can devise a card that expresses this level of love. God's love has been expressed in a unique and powerful way.

Not only did God send Jesus, Jesus also gave us the Lord's Supper. Like an anniversary card, it reminds us of God's commitment and sacrifice. Better than a card, we participate in a deeply meaningful act of sharing. Let us join together now in an expression of God's love.

Worship the Worthy

Then I saw in the right hand of him who sat on the throne a scroll with writing on both sides and sealed with seven seals. And I saw a mighty angel proclaiming in a loud voice, "Who is worthy to break the seals and open the scroll?" But no one in heaven or on earth or under the earth could open the scroll or even look inside it. I wept and wept because no one was found who was worthy to open the scroll or look inside. Then one of the elders said to me, "Do not weep! See, the Lion of the tribe of Judah, the Root of David, has triumphed. He is able to open the scroll and its seven seals." Then I saw a Lamb, looking as if it had been slain, standing in the center of the throne, encircled by the four living creatures and the elders. He had seven horns and seven eyes, which are the seven spirits of God sent out into all the earth. Revelation 5:1–6

This picture of heaven from Revelation demonstrates an important principle: the worthy are worshiped.

Sports superstars attract fans because of superb talent. They are above average. Media hype alone can't attract a large following. Fans are attracted to the best in the sport. That's why the legends of baseball are Babe Ruth, Roger Maris, and Mark McGwire. They deserve recognition for their exploits on the field.

Jesus also attracts our attention. But he is far more than a sports hero. He is the Son of God who died for us. This fact makes him worthy of worship. We memorialize his great sacrifice with this simple observance.

Recipe for a Good Meditation

Ingredients:
1 Scripture
1 Main Point
1 Main Illustration

Combine Scripture, main point
and illustration with prayer.

Trim to a single bite-sized serving.

Serve with warmth and a smile.

How to Use the *Ideas* Sections

You are the key to delivering effective meditations. I strongly believe that you have interesting stories and ideas to use. This section will help you discover and tap the illustrations in your own life.

Each topic in these sections highlights a principle related to the offering or communion. Each topic contains four parts. First, a key verse containing the principle is quoted.

Second, one or more references to other Scripture passages that teach the principle are included.

Third, the *Points* list in each topic gives choices of several main points that could be made. As you read and reflect on the Scriptures you may think of more. Select one main point to emphasize.

Fourth, the *Illustration* list gives starter ideas for stories and illustrations. Rather than just reading these items in your meditations, use them to bring your own experiences to mind. Personal illustrations and true stories are highly effective. Several examples used in this book came from my personal experience. You also have some great stories that can be used for meditations. Let the illustration starters help you find them.

Mix and match these elements to create your own meditations. Remember the formula: use one Scripture and one illustration to make one point.

This list can also help you keep variety. Try highlighting a different principle each time you give a meditation.

The references used here do not exhaust the supply for the offering or the Lord's Supper. Literally dozens of passages teach about the death of Jesus. Passages describing Jesus' death or explaining its meaning can also be used for the Lord's Supper. The Bible also contains examples of people presenting offerings to God. Many of these can be used for offering meditations.

Ideas for Offering Meditations

OFFERING: OWNERS AND MANAGERS

"Again, it will be like a man going on a journey, who called his servants and entrusted his property to them." Matthew 25:14
Matthew 25:14–30; Psalm 24:1–2; 1 Corinthians 6:19–20

Points

1. God owns all things because he created all things.
2. We are managers of God's wealth.
3. We are accountable for managing God's wealth.
4. We belong to God because he created us and saved us.

Illustrations

1. Tell about renting a house or object. Rent is due the owner. The offering, though not the same as rent, recognizes the ownership of God.
2. Owners want their possessions to please them. Tell about an auto you owned that was a lemon. Tell about one you own that pleases you. We are God's possessions. We should please God with our lives. He has invested a lot in us. What kind of return is he getting on his investment?

3. Tell about borrowing a pickup truck, lawn mower, boat, or another item. When you returned the item, did you fill the tank with gas or offer money? Gratitude for using something that belongs to another is often expressed by giving a gift. God is the owner of all we use. Express your gratitude with a gift.

4. Tell about a time you regretted loaning an item to someone. How was it misused? Tell about the lack of gratitude. Relate this to God's granting us life and resources. Are we using them correctly? Are we displaying a lack of gratitude?

5. Ask for a show of hands on these questions: "How many of you own your own business? How many of you are employees?" Point out how an employee is accountable for using work hours and the employer's resources (equipment, capital, etc.) to benefit the company. Relate this to Christians using their time, talent and treasure to benefit Christ.

OFFERING: GIVE TO GROW

"Now he who supplies seed to the sower and bread for food will also supply and increase your store of seed and will enlarge the harvest of your righteousness." 2 Corinthians 9:10
Matthew 19:16–21; Galatians 6:7–10

Points

1. Give generously and you harvest righteousness.
2. You will never fully mature until you give generously.
3. The more you give, the more you grow.
4. Do you feel something is missing in your relationship with God? It could be giving.
5. To grow, give enough to please the Spirit, not what pleases the flesh.

Illustrations

1. Physical fitness requires effort. Energy must be expended in exercise. Self-discipline must be used to eat properly. Tell about your efforts in this area. Christian growth is the same. It requires effort in different areas. One area is the self-discipline required to give generously.

2. Tell about a vague uneasiness you've had because you were "missing something." This may involve packing for a vacation, work responsibilities, tasting a new recipe, or something else. Relate this to the feeling of the young man in Matthew 19. Ask people if they sense something missing in their relationship to God. It could be they need to give away more of what they have.

3. Ask if people are ever torn between two desires. Examples could be the desire for fattening foods and the desire to eat healthy foods. Whichever desire they follow, they will reap the result of their choice. The same is true with tithing. People either surrender to the desire to keep the money, or they follow the higher desire to tithe. Only one choice leads to healthy spiritual growth.

4. Talk about teaching children to be responsible. Examples could be making the bed, brushing their teeth, or observing a curfew. Children do not mature until they are responsible. Christians also need to mature. They must be responsible about presenting offerings to God.

OFFERING: MONEY IS NO SUBSTITUTE

"Woe to you, teachers of the law and Pharisees, you hypocrites! You give a tenth of your spices—mint, dill and cummin. But you have neglected the more important matters of the law—justice, mercy and faithfulness. You should have practiced the latter, without neglecting the former." Matthew 23:23

Hosea 6:6; Matthew 9:12–13; Luke 18:9–14

Points

1. Tithing is not a substitute for love.
2. Tithing is not a substitute for obedience.
3. Pride in your giving is wrong.
4. Jesus praised tithing but condemned hypocrisy.

Illustrations

1. Tell about your favorite quiz game or quiz-style game show. Explain that you have an important quiz for them today. The question: "Name the one thing the Pharisees did that Jesus praised." The answer: tithing.

2. Tell about a time you unsuccessfully tried to substitute one thing for another. Examples might be a quick smile when your spouse wanted conversation and attention, a copied school assignment, a bad check for cash, etc. Praise people for tithing and giving. Then warn them that it is not a substitute for doing everything else that Jesus commanded.

3. Tell about a time pride ruined something. Possible examples include: someone's ego ruining a friendship, the failure to admit an error which damaged a relationship or career, an evening ruined by someone's haughty attitude, etc. Relate this to the offering. The offering is a special time when we show love and faith to God. Don't let pride ruin it.

4. Tell about a time your child tried to "be nice" while disobeying you. Explain how politeness does not replace obedience. Explain how a nice offering does not replace obeying God. Ask people to examine not just their habit of giving, but their obedience to the Lord.

5. The usual definition of *hypocrite* is someone who says one thing but does another. Jesus' definition is different: one who does the right thing but has the wrong attitude. Note Jesus praising the Pharisees for tithing as well as condemning their attitude. Relate this to the worshipers—don't just present an offering; present a clean heart.

OFFERING: A MATTER OF HEART

"Each man should give what he has decided in his heart to give, not reluctantly or under compulsion, for God loves a cheerful giver." 2 Corinthians 9:7

Points

1. Christians don't "have to" tithe, they "get to" tithe.
2. What you give reflects what's in your heart.
3. You decide what you want to give.
4. Jesus measures your offering by the percentage amount, not the dollar amount.

Illustrations

1. Tell about leaving a tip at a restaurant. Explain that some people are very faithful to figure the proper percentage for the tip. They want to be fair to the waitress. Explain that some people are more concerned about tipping waitresses than they are about tithing to the Lord. Good waitresses deserve the tip. The good Lord deserves the tithe. Urge people to give a tithe.

2. If you buy a cup of coffee and leave a dollar tip, the waitress is probably pleased. If you order a complete dinner for six people, including dessert and several refills of drinks and rolls, and leave the same dollar tip, the waitress is probably insulted. The message is not in the dollar amount, but the percentage amount of the tip. The same is true of your offering. What message do you want to send?

3. Tell about losing something and offering a reward. Why is the reward offered? It is not required. It is offered to express our gratitude that others worked to find what was lost. We also present offerings to the Lord out of gratitude. If you appreciate what God has done for you, you will present an offering to him.

4. Have everyone open his wallet or her purse. Ask the following questions: "Do you believe God is almighty? Do you believe that God can bless your life? Do you believe God can increase your income?" Explain that God promises to increase the income of those who trust him by tithing and generous giving. Read either Malachi 3:10 or 2 Corinthians 9:7–11.

5. Tell about buying an engagement ring. Explain how you wanted to get the prettiest, biggest ring. Explain that you weren't motivated to buy it out of obligation, but out of love. Explain how tithing is not done from a sense of obligation, but from love.

OFFERING: LOSE TO KEEP

"For whoever wants to save his life will lose it, but whoever loses his life for me will save it." Luke 9:24

Luke 9:23–25; Matthew 10:37–39; Matthew 16:24–26; Mark 8:34–37; John 12:25–26

Points

1. When it comes to the offering, are you denying yourself?
2. Only what you give to Jesus will you truly keep.
3. Make the choice: your money or your life?
4. You can't follow Jesus without denying yourself.

Illustrations

1. How would you respond if someone pulled a gun and demanded your money or your life? Most would give up their wallet. Some would try to wrestle the gun away. Jesus is not holding a gun, but his message is similar. Will you give up your life and your money, or try to keep both?
2. Ask the following: "Where in American culture are we encouraged to deny ourselves? Can you think of one TV commercial

asking you to do this?" List several commercials that have the opposite message. Then ask people to listen to Jesus. Read Luke 9:23–25.

3. Tell about a heroic act you've seen in which someone denied himself. Tell about the admiration and approval this act generated. Explain how the person followed a higher motive than selfishness. Explain that Jesus requires us to put his interests above our own. One way we express this is in the offering.

4. Talk about something you really wanted to protect and what you did to keep it safe. Examples could be money in the bank, a classic car, family heirlooms, etc. Make the point that the most precious thing to protect is your life. To save it, you give it away to Jesus. Ask: "Does the gift you now bring in worship show that you've given your life away?"

5. Hold up a Chinese finger puzzle. Demonstrate how your fingers go in easy, but can't be pulled out. The harder you try the more it hurts. Show how to get your fingers out by pushing the puzzle together to release its grip. The same is true with life. The more one lives for self and seeks to save self, the more injury will result. Encourage people to do the opposite, to give themselves to Jesus. Their offerings should express the surrender of their lives to Christ.

Offering: First Fruits

"Honor the LORD with your wealth, with the firstfruits of all your crops; then your barns will be filled to overflowing, and your vats will brim over with new wine." Proverbs 3:9–10

2 Chronicles 31:5; Exodus 34:26a; Nehemiah 10:37

Points

1. God deserves and desires the first portion of our income.
2. Giving to God is our highest financial priority.
3. God is honored when we make our offering the first priority.
4. Put God first and he will bless you.

Illustrations

1. Talk about receiving several bills in the mail. How does one decide which bill to pay first? Usually the decision involves gaining the greatest advantage by avoiding the largest interest or penalties. The obligation to put God first gives the greatest advantage of all. Honoring God is the first "bill" we should pay, because he will bless us.

2. Tell about having an important guest in your home for dinner. Explain how the guest was honored. You might describe: offering the best seat, offering first choice of the main course, being served dessert first, etc. Explain that making our offering the first in our financial priorities treats God with the honor he deserves.

3. Tell about a time you saw children arguing over who should be first—first in line for a church dinner, first in line to go to recess, first to receive candy or a treat, etc. Show how adults can also be childish by spending money on themselves first and on God last.

4. Ask people if they recognize what is most important. Ask several questions such as: "Which is more important, your money or your life? A new boat or the operation your child needs? A good education or a good wardrobe? A big house or tithing?" Explain how many people do not see tithing as a priority. Then explain Proverbs 3:9–10.

5. Tell about a time you got in trouble by failing to do something important. Examples might be filling the car with gas, depositing money in your checking account, turning the oven on to bake something, etc. First things must come first. Relate how our failure to make God first financially can cause us trouble.

OFFERING: CHEERFULNESS

"Each man should give what he has decided in his heart to give, not reluctantly or under compulsion, for God loves a cheerful giver." 2 Corinthians 9:7

2 Corinthians 9:6–8

Points

1. God is delighted when you give joyously.
2. God wants you to give from the heart, not out of duty.
3. Look in your heart, not in your wallet, to decide how much to give.
4. Give until it feels good.
5. The offering is a time of happiness for you and God.

Illustrations

1. Imagine a wife, feeling tender-hearted, saying to her husband, "I love you."
The husband replies, "I *have to* love you too."
"What?" she asks.

"Well, the Bible commands husbands to love their wives. I have no choice, I have to love you."

Would any wife be pleased with this? She doesn't want to be loved out of obligation. Neither does God. He doesn't want us giving an offering out of obligation either. Give what's in your heart.

2. The wedding is beautiful. The candles are lit. The couple exchanges vows. The minister says, "You may kiss the bride."

The groom replies, "Oh, do I *have to?*"

A ludicrous picture isn't it? It is just as ludicrous for a Christian to think, "Do I have to give an offering?" Offerings flow from the love of God and joy in your heart.

3. Tell about buying an engagement ring or other gift of love. Explain how you wanted to buy it. Tell how you scrimped, saved, and/or borrowed to buy the most lavish gift you could. The amount you spent didn't depend on the spare change in your wallet, but on the love in your heart. Apply this to the decision of how much to give in the offering.

4. Tell about one of your happiest times in life which was shared with someone else. Tell of the closeness you felt. Relate this to the offering. It should be a time of happiness for you and God. It should be a time of sharing.

5. Tell about a time you received joy because of a good thing done for another. Examples could be the joy of watching children or grandchildren open gifts, kindness to a neighbor in need, etc. Relate this to the offering. It is a weekly time of joy in giving to God.

Offering: God Gives More

"Give, and it will be given to you. A good measure, pressed down, shaken together and running over, will be poured into your lap. For with the measure you use, it will be measured to you." Luke 6:38

Luke 12:26–31; Matthew 6:24–33; Malachi 3:10; 2 Corinthians 9:6; 2 Corinthians 9:10–11

Points

1. When you give, God gives more.
2. Your measure of giving is also your measure of receiving.
3. You can't outgive God.
4. Here's a sure thing: God blesses those who give.
5. God is generous with the generous.

Illustrations

1. Tell about a time in your life when God blessed you beyond expectation. Explain how God treats us better than we deserve. God always gives more to us than we give to him.
2. Tell about the most unexpected and lavish Christmas gift you have received. Relate the giver's desire to give joy through the

gift to God's desire to bless our lives. Explain that those who give generously to God will not be forgotten. God will meet our needs and pour out blessings on us.

3. Use beans or seeds, a small cup, a large coffee can, small pail and large pan to provide the following object lesson. Fill the pail, cup and coffee can with seed. Hold the cup over the large pan and empty it. (You may need another to assist you.) Say something like this: "Your measure of giving is your measure of receiving. Give a small amount and you will receive it back with more." Carefully fill the empty cup from the pail. When full, allow a little extra to overflow and fall into the pan. Now explain God's promise: "If you give much,...[*empty the coffee can*] God will give you more. [*Rapidly fill the can from the pail, allowing a large amount to overflow.*] Why not give according to the size of blessing you'd like to receive?"

4. Talk about an area of life where running out of money is disastrous. Examples might be political campaigns, new businesses, personal budgets, vacations, etc. Explain how many people don't give much because they worry about running out of money. Point to God's promise to supply their need. Remind them that they can't give more than God. He never runs out of resources.

5. Most people are leery of losing their money. Promises of a sure thing, whether a winning horse, a hot stock tip, or real estate venture are met with skepticism. Con men bilk people with promises of a "sure thing." God is not running a con. You do not lose money when you offer it to him. Here is a sure thing: God blesses those who give to him.

Offering: Flow of Wealth

"As it is written: 'He has scattered abroad his gifts to the poor; his righteousness endures forever.' Now he who supplies seed to the sower and bread for food will also supply and increase your store of seed and will enlarge the harvest of your righteousness. You will be made rich in every way so that you can be generous on every occasion, and through us your generosity will result in thanksgiving to God." 2 Corinthians 9:10–11

2 Corinthians 9:6–11

Points

1. God supplies your wealth.
2. God can increase your wealth.
3. God grants wealth to the generous.
4. Your generosity brings thanksgiving to God.
5. God *promises* to supply and increase the wealth you use in generosity.

Illustrations

1. Tell about watching a river flow. Explain that wealth is like a river. It flows into your life and God wants it to flow out. When you are generous, God increases the flow.

2. Wealth is like seed. Plant seed and it produces a harvest. Give your money generously and it also produces a harvest. You harvest more seed. God harvests thanksgiving.

3. In the Lord's Prayer we ask for daily bread. God grants us opportunities, skills, and money to earn a living. But God also provides "daily seed." God provides opportunities, skills, and money to give away. Part of your wealth is "bread"—God intends it to supply your need. Part of your wealth is "seed"—God intends it to supply the needs of others. Plant your seed.

4. Use bean seed in a clear plastic bag to present this object lesson. Ask the question, "How many beans do I have? Twenty? Thirty?" Explain that you have an unlimited supply. "Don't see what exists—see what *can be*. See this as a bag of seed, not of beans. If you plant and harvest it, and keep planting part of it, it never runs out." Direct the people to open and look into their checkbooks or wallets. Ask, "How much money do you have? Do you say to yourself, 'I don't have enough to give'? No, no, don't see what exists—see what *can be*. Your money is seed. Give your money and God gives you back more. God wants you to keep planting, to give and keep giving. He promises to make it possible."

Offering: God or Mammon

"No one can serve two masters. Either he will hate the one and love the other, or he will be devoted to the one and despise the other. You cannot serve both God and Money." Matthew 6:24

Matthew 6:19–21; Mark 4:18–19; Luke 12:15–21; 1 Timothy 6:6–10; 1 Timothy 6:17–19

Points

1. Serve God with your money, or serve money without God.
2. We all want to be rich. The question is rich in wealth or rich toward God?
3. Love money and you will be trapped.
4. Love God, not money, and you will enjoy life.

Illustrations

1. Use a large fishing lure to teach an object lesson. Show how a lure deceives fish. They think it is something good and get hooked. If they can't get off, they will probably be eaten by the fisherman. 1 Timothy 6:9–10 says those who love money are trapped and pierced, much like a fish on a hook. A measure of

93

whether you love God or money is the tithe. Urge those who do not tithe to "get free" before they perish.

2. Tell about a time when "getting more" made you miserable. Examples might be overeating, borrowing beyond your means, headaches from watching too much TV, etc. Most don't realize that trying to get more money will make them miserable. Giving more money makes life more enjoyable. 1 Timothy 6:17–18 says God provides for our enjoyment, but we must give and share.

3. Explain how the idea of "getting rich" captures our attention. Examples might be the lottery, casinos, television game shows, etc. Everyone wants to be rich. The question is what kind of riches—riches toward God or money?

4. Tell about a time you were stuck between competing interests. Examples to consider are trying to hold down two jobs, trying to date two people, a demanding job and the needs of your family, etc. Describe the problems this caused. Show how you eventually solved the problems by abandoning one of the competing interests. Relate this to the love of God and the love of money.

5. Talk about the differences you experience in relationships to your boss and your subordinates at work. Show how you serve one while the others serve under you. One example might be to whom you can say no. If you really serve God, can you say no to giving an offering?

6. Give an example of devotion. It might be a friend's care for a dying spouse, a friend's care for a handicapped child, a volunteer at a nursing home, etc. Are you devoted to God or material things? Devotion to God means you never miss tithing each source of income.

Ideas for Communion Meditations

Lord's Supper: A Contract With God

"This is my blood of the covenant, which is poured out for many for the forgiveness of sins."
Matthew 26:28

Matthew 26:26–29; Mark 14:22–25; Luke 22:14–20; 1 Corinthians 11:23–30; Hebrews 9:15

Points

1. Our forgiveness relies on God's love *and* on a contract.
2. God has made a treaty of peace with us.
3. We remember one of the oldest and most honored agreements in history.
4. We share in the best deal that has ever been made.

Illustrations

1. Tell about a contract you have signed that promised a future completion. Examples might be closing on your home, paying for the future delivery of goods, or a business deal. Did you ever reread the contract? Did you ever consult the contract to reassure yourself you'd receive what was stipulated? The Lord's

Supper reminds us of a contract for the future blessing of eternal life.

2. In 1783 the Treaty of Paris ended the war between Great Britain and the American Colonies. Over a hundred years later, the two nations who had once been enemies became the closest of allies in the two World Wars. What we remember through the Lord's Supper is a covenant. Much like a treaty, we have ceased to be enemies of God and are now close to him.

3. Ask: "Have you ever said these words: 'I want it in writing'?" Tell about a time you wanted an agreement in writing. Explain that the reason for seeking a written agreement is to verify it in the future. The Lord's supper represents an agreement that can be verified. But it is not an agreement in writing, but one in blood. It reminds us of promises God has made to forgive us.

4. Briefly tell about a good deal you made. Examples might be a lucrative business deal, negotiating a favorable price on your home, buying something at auction. Tell how the best deal ever made was forgiveness through Christ. Explain how God made a covenant, or contract, through Jesus' death. Explain how the Lord's Supper reminds us of the greatest agreement ever made.

5. Briefly tell about making a motel reservation and receiving a confirmation number. The confirmation number serves as proof you made the reservation. The Lord's Supper is similar. Jesus provided forgiveness through his death. In essence, he made reservations for us in heaven. He gave us the Lord's Supper as proof the reservations have been made.

Lord's Supper: Do This to Remember

"And when he had given thanks, he broke it and said, 'This is my body, which is for you; do this in remembrance of me.'" 1 Corinthians 11:24

Luke 22:14–20; 1 Corinthians 11:23–30

Points

1. Do this to remember Jesus.
2. Remember, Christ died for you.
3. Remember the death of Christ and its meaning for you

Illustrations

1. Show a photo of something or someone you enjoy remembering. Examples might be your wedding, a favorite vacation, a deceased loved one, etc. Tell about the good feeling you receive from looking at the photo. Explain how the Lord's Supper also gives a good feeling because it reminds us of Jesus' death.
2. Show a souvenir you got from a vacation or trip. Explain how the souvenir brings to mind all the details and events from the

trip. Relate this to the Lord's Supper. Explain how this simple meal reminds us of Jesus' life, death, resurrection, etc.

3. Tell about the customary way you observe your wedding anniversary. (For example, some couples always go out to eat, look through the photo album, etc.) Explain that the Lord's Supper is a weekly anniversary that marks Jesus' death for us.

4. Holidays are often dedicated to the memory of great individuals. We have holidays that remember George Washington, Abraham Lincoln, and Dr. Martin Luther King, Jr. We also have holidays that remember the countless individuals who have fought for our freedom, such as Memorial Day, Veterans Day, and the Fourth of July. We also have holidays that remember our Lord Jesus. One is in December, one in the Spring, and one is observed each week at the Lord's Table. We do this to remember him.

5. Tell about a time you placed flowers on a grave. Explain how this act honored the memory of the person. Relate how the Lord's Supper also honors the memory of Jesus. But, unlike flowers on a grave, it reminds us of the one who died and yet lives again.

LORD'S SUPPER: FORGIVE, OR FORGIVEN?

"This is my blood of the covenant, which is poured out for many for the forgiveness of sins."
Matthew 26:28
Matthew 26:26–29

Points

1. We do not gather to be forgiven, but to remember our forgiveness.
2. God has already punished your sins in Christ's death.
3. Forgiveness is an incredibly high value.
4. The price of forgiveness is high.

Illustration

1. Tell about getting your property taxes paid. Explain how the clerk stamps the receipt as paid. Explain how the Lord's Supper reminds us that the price for our forgiveness has been paid.
2. Briefly tell about your wedding. Explain that a couple gets married once, but celebrates their anniversary every year. Observing the anniversary isn't even necessary to keep the marriage legally

intact. The Lord's Supper is similar. It is not required to keep us forgiven. It commemorates the death of Christ which accomplished that forgiveness.

3. Tell about a time you participated in a celebration of repaying a large debt. Examples might be paying off your house, a church mortgage, or a business debt. Explain that the Lord's Supper is the celebration of a debt paid—the debt of our sins paid by Jesus' death.

4. Tell about your favorite way to observe the Fourth of July. Explain how the holiday celebrates the freedom of our nation. Explain how the Lord's Supper celebrates our freedom from sin.

5. Some of the most important things in our lives are quite expensive. Homes and cars are examples. So is lifesaving treatment when our health is threatened. Our forgiveness also cost a tremendous amount. Today we remember the price paid for our forgiveness, the death of Jesus on the cross.

LORD'S SUPPER: PROCLAIM HIS DEATH

"For whenever you eat this bread and drink this cup, you proclaim the Lord's death until he comes." 1 Corinthians 11:26
1 Corinthians 11:23–30; 1 Peter 2:9–10

Points

1. This is an act of praise.
2. This is a witness to the world.
3. This is a gospel sermon.
4. This is a broadcast of God's love.

Illustrations

1. Show a cap or t-shirt from your favorite team. Explain how fans proudly announce their loyalty through wearing such items. Relate this to the Lord's Supper. Explain how the observance of the Supper proclaims your loyalty to Jesus. It also proclaims the reason for your loyalty, namely, his death for you.
2. Tell about visiting a carnival, fair, or ball park where vendors constantly called to people to buy their wares. Explain how the

Lord's Supper is also a proclamation, not of something to buy, but of the gift of forgiveness given by God through Jesus.

3. Display print advertising that makes a free offer for something. Explain how the offers for free items attract attention. Relate this to the Lord's Supper. The Supper attracts attention because it proclaims Jesus' death and the free gift of eternal life.

4. Tell about seeing graffiti on walls, bridges, or other places. Explain why people paint graffiti, namely, to proclaim something. Maybe they proclaim their love, their loyalty to a gang, or just their existence. Explain how the Lord's Supper is not graffiti, but it also proclaims love, loyalty and existence. It proclaims God's love for us displayed in Jesus death. Our participation declares our loyalty to Christ. It also proclaims the existence of Jesus and the historical reality of his death and resurrection.

5. Broadcasting covers a wide area. Tower transmitters send signals over thousands of square miles. A single satellite can broadcast to huge sections of the globe. But nothing beats the broadcasting power of the communion service. Through countless Christians in hundreds of thousands of churches spread across every populated continent, this simple observance declares the gospel message. As you partake today, you join this powerful, global witness to Christ's death.

Lord's Supper: Facets of Fellowship

"Is not the cup of thanksgiving for which we give thanks a participation in the blood of Christ? And is not the bread that we break a participation in the body of Christ?" 1 Corinthians 10:16
1 Corinthians 10:16–21

Points

1. Participating in this Supper unites us in fellowship.
2. We share this Supper with Jesus.
3. Eating this reminds us that we worship Jesus, and only Jesus.
4. We gather around this table with a special closeness to God and each other.

Illustrations

1. Tell about a time you became a closer friend to someone through a common experience. Examples might be fishing, hunting, or recreation. Relate this to participation in the communion. Explain how this common experience with our Savior makes us closer to him.

2. Tell about the camaraderie you have experienced as part of a team, military squad, or club. Explain how the closeness you felt was related to common goals, experiences, and rituals. Relate this to the Lord's Supper. Explain how we have one Lord, a common faith, common baptism, common mission (to serve Jesus), and a common ritual—the Lord's Supper.

3. Tell about going to a family reunion and the sense of kinship you experienced, even with relatives you hardly knew. Explain how the Lord's Supper is like a spiritual family reunion. Explain how we have a kinship even if we don't know each other well.

4. Have you ever dreamed of hitting a home run or of catching the touchdown pass? Many of us dream of being in the game, not in the stands. We want to be a part of greatness. We just want to be on the team. We long to feel the thrill of victory. The Lord's Supper reminds us that we *participate* with Christ. We are a part of greatness. We belong together with him. We have a great victory. Feel that thrill as you partake today.

5. Tell about voting in a presidential election. Remind people that a person only receives one vote. He or she can't vote for a second candidate or vote in another precinct. Explain that the Lord's Supper reminds us that we only have one Lord. We can't worship any other, or join in worship celebrations for other religions.

LORD'S SUPPER: EXAMINE YOURSELF

"A man ought to examine himself before he eats of the bread and drinks of the cup." 1 Corinthians 11:28
1 Corinthians 11:23–30

Points

1. This is a dangerous practice for the unprepared.
2. Take this time to examine yourself.
3. Examine your relationship to the Lord and his body.
4. Think about how you do this.

Illustrations

1. Tell about a flight you've taken in a small plane. Describe how the pilot used a pre-flight checklist. Explain that the reason for the checklist is safety. Relate this to examining yourself before partaking of communion. Suggest three or four checklist items for people to use, such as the following questions: Is your conscience clear with God, or do you need to clear it? Are your relationships with others, especially Christians, good or in need of repair? Is your mind focused on Jesus, or is it distracted?

2. Talk about a physical checkup where vital signs are taken. The vital signs give an indicator of health or sickness. Urge people to take their spiritual vital signs before partaking together. Have them examine the way they are treating fellow Christians.

3. Talk about someone's visit to a health fair and how the screening tests discovered a problem. Examples might be unexpectedly high blood pressure or cholesterol. Explain how these conditions, if left undiagnosed, could lead to serious health problems. Relate this to the Lord's Supper. Explain how the failure to examine ourselves may lead to serious spiritual health problems.

4. Explain how an audit works. It is a detailed look at all the accounts. Urge people to give themselves a spiritual audit. Urge them to take a detailed look at their loyalty to Christ and their love for other Christians before partaking of the Lord's Supper.

5. Many manufacturing processes have quality control inspectors. Through the use of machines and/or people, the products are checked to insure they meet the standards. Maybe you've removed scraps of paper from your clothes that said something like, "Inspected by #21." To have a quality product, it must be examined. The same is true for us. If we want to be quality Christians, and to have a quality experience observing communion, we must examine ourselves. As you wait to be served today, ask yourself one question: "Is there anything in my life that is destroying the holiness Christ is developing in me?"

LORD'S SUPPER: YOUR PLEDGE

"This is my blood of the covenant, which is poured out for many for the forgiveness of sins."
Matthew 26:28
Matthew 26:26–29; Mark 14:22–25; Luke 22:14–20; 1 Corinthians 11:23–30; Hebrews 9:15

Points

1. Jesus made a promise to us. Do you remember your promise to him?
2. Let the Lord's Supper shape your self-image.
3. You affirm your loyalty to Christ when you eat and drink this communion.

Illustrations

1. Display a wedding ring. Explain that the unending circle of gold is a symbol of the unending love and commitment of two people in a Christian marriage. Explain that the Lord's Supper is also a symbol of the pledge of unending love and commitment made between Christ and each Christian.

2. Have you seen news reports of the President signing a bill into law? He usually signs several copies and hands the pens he uses to people instrumental in passing the bill. The pen then becomes a symbol and reminder of each person's dedication to the legislative victory. Communion is also a symbol of victory. It reminds us of Jesus' death and our forgiveness. It should also remind us of the dedication we have pledged to Jesus.

3. Adults in the Boy Scouts of America attend advanced training called Wood Badge. There they make a commitment to serve within Scouting. After they fulfill the commitment, which usually involves several goals and time of service, they receive a wooden emblem to wear. The emblem reaffirms their loyalty and commitment. Likewise, the Lord's Supper is an emblem of Jesus' loyalty and commitment. By partaking we also reaffirm our commitment to be loyal and serve him.

4. Tell about saying the Pledge of Allegiance when you went to school. Explain how reciting the pledge helped shape your views of yourself as an American. Relate this to the Lord's Supper. Explain how it constantly shapes our view of ourselves. Emphasize one of the following concepts: We are sinners saved by grace. We are not our own; we've been bought with a price (1 Corinthians 6:19–20). We have denied ourselves to live for Christ (Matthew 16:24).

5. The old hymn says "I'll live for him who died for me, how happy then my life shall be." The Lord's Supper reminds us of death and life. We remember Jesus' death for us. We should also remember our deaths. He agreed to die for us, then he lived again. We have agreed to die to self, and then to live for him. This is the nature of a covenant. Each party promises something. How well are you doing in your promise to live for Christ?

Lord's Supper: Giving of Thanks

"Is not the cup of thanksgiving for which we give thanks a participation in the blood of Christ? And is not the bread that we break a participation in the body of Christ?" 1 Corinthians 10:16

Matthew 26:26–29; Mark 14:22–25; Luke 22:14–20; 1 Corinthians 10:16–17; 1 Corinthians 11:23–30

Points

1. Be thankful for Christ's sacrifice on your behalf.
2. Use this time to express your thankfulness to your Savior.
3. The gift of Jesus' life is so big we must keep thanking him.

Illustrations

1. Show a thank you card. It is a simple way to express thanks. Relate it to the Lord's Supper, which is also a way we remember Christ and express thanks for his sacrifice.
2. Tell about a time you felt extremely thankful to another person. Examples might be receiving a lavish and unexpected gift, someone finding your lost child or pet, etc. Tell how you felt

and how you expressed that thankfulness. Remind people that this emotion is natural in observing the Lord's Supper.

3. There are many songs of thanksgiving, such as "Thank You, Lord," "Give Thanks," or "Count Your Blessings." We also give prayers of thanksgiving. But did you know that the communion is a cup of thanksgiving? When Jesus instituted the Lord's Supper he gave thanks. Today, as we observe it, we also give thanks to God for saving us from the penalty of our sin.

4. Tell about a time you did not receive the thanks and recognition you deserved. Describe your disappointment. Relate this to God's expectation for our thankfulness for sending Christ. Urge people to offer prayers of thanksgiving as they partake of communion.

5. What parent has not wished to make his or her child less selfish? One powerful way to do this is to teach children to be thankful. The act of writing thank you notes and of giving the polite words, "thank you," develop humility. Children learn to recognize those who bless their lives. Our heavenly Father also wants us to be less selfish. The Lord's Supper teaches us to be constantly thankful for the sacrifice of Christ. In it we humbly recognize the true source of blessing and goodness in our lives.

Lord's Supper: Worthy Manner

"Therefore, whoever eats the bread or drinks the cup of the Lord in an unworthy manner will be guilty of sinning against the body and blood of the Lord." 1 Corinthians 11:27

1 Corinthians 11:23–30

Points

1. Do not partake unless you do so in a worthy manner .
2. The Lord's body (the church) must be treated with respect.
3. We are not worthy of Christ's death, no one is. Our focus is observing this in a worthy manner.
4. Taking the Lord's Supper may be one of the most dangerous things you do.

Illustration

1. Tell about the most valuable work of art you have seen. Explain how carefully it was treated and about the level of security around it. Relate this to the Lord's Supper. Explain that we must be careful in how we observe it. Explain that we must treat the observance and our fellow worshipers with respect.

2. Have you ever received a gift you did not deserve? Perhaps you tried to refuse it. Maybe, since the giver insisted, you accepted it humbly. Surely you did not insult the giver and hurl the gift to the ground! Even when receiving an undeserved gift, we treat the gift and giver with respect. The Lord's Supper reminds us of God's gift of his Son. We don't deserve it. We will never deserve it. 1 Corinthians doesn't teach us to be worthy of Christ, but to treat the symbol of the gift in a worthy manner.

3. Tell about someone who acted inappropriately at a wedding. Explain how others were affected by the bad behavior. Give an example or two of rules of behavior at weddings. Possible examples follow: don't say bad things about the bride, don't criticize the decorations or food, and don't make a big scene with your ex-spouse. Explain there are also rules of behavior for observing the Lord's Supper. It must be observed in a worthy manner.

4. Imagine a funeral. You're seated as the service begins. Imagine the speaker, standing at the head of the casket, telling horrible, slanderous things about the deceased. Wouldn't you be shocked? Why? Because the person was acting in a totally unacceptable way. Relate this to the Lord's Supper. We must be sure we observe it in an acceptable way.

5. All of us have seen a beauty queen such as Miss America on television. All beauty queens have something in common—they are all under contract. They must behave in certain ways, stipulated in the contract. If they act in an unbecoming way, they will be stripped of the title. We must also be careful in the way we act as Christians, especially in relation to the communion. If we partake in an unbecoming way, we may eat and drink judgment upon ourselves.

LORD'S SUPPER: A MATTER OF HEALTH

"That is why many among you are weak and sick, and a number of you have fallen asleep." 1 Corinthians 11:30
 1 Corinthians 11:23–30

Points

1. The Lord's Supper is linked to your physical health.
2. Spiritual problems in the church can cause physical problems for you.
3. The Lord's Supper is far more important than we first think.
4. You're really careful with your physical health. You should be as careful with the Lord's Supper.

Illustrations

1. Tell about a diet you have observed for health reasons. Tell about the dangers if you break the diet. Explain that the Lord's Supper is also related to physical health. Those who partake in an unworthy manner may suffer physical health problems.
2. Tell about your efforts to develop a healthy habit of exercise. Stress that the key to any benefit is regular exercise. Explain

that the regular observance of the Lord's Supper is good for our spiritual health and may also be linked to our physical health.

3. Modern medical research has shown that our mental attitude is linked to our physical health. Certain attitudes place people at a higher risk for ulcer, high blood pressure, and heart disease. Perhaps the way the Lord's Supper is linked to our health involves our mental attitude. People at Corinth had sinful attitudes toward each other while observing the Lord's Supper. By treating each other with disrespect, they were disrespecting Christ. The communion gives us an opportunity to set our hearts straight in our relationship with God and each other. Before you partake today, get your heart right with God. If necessary, go to others and get things right with them.

4. Tell about the way you work to protect your health. Examples might be diet, exercise, health screening, regular check-ups, etc. Explain that we should extend this same type of effort to the way we observe communion. Explain that the proper attitudes in this observance protect our spiritual and physical health.

5. Tell about toxins that can poison people. Examples could be chemical wastes, radioactivity, or contaminated food. Explain the damage that exposure to these toxins can cause. Urge people to be rid of any toxic attitudes they have toward Christ, communion, or their fellow man before partaking of the Lord's Supper.

ABOUT THE AUTHOR

Elmer Fuller is a husband, father, minister, author, and adjunct instructor at St. Louis Christian College. He has a bachelor's degree in Christian ministry and a master's degree in theology. He has served in full-time ministry since 1983. In 1992, with the help of Missouri Operation for Vigorous Evangelism, he started the church where he now serves as the minister.

He has been published over a dozen times in national Christian magazines. He has also authored the *Celebration of Friendship Ministry Kit* available from http://grow.faithweb.com.

CELEBRATION OF FRIENDSHIP MINISTRY KIT

The *Celebration of Friendship Ministry Kit* is a complete, customized program enabling you to conduct a 30-day emphasis on friendship issues ending in a large attendance day. Especially geared to small and medium-sized churches, this kit is customized to each church—saving valuable time and money for busy ministry professionals.

Church members who participate commit themselves to do 10 actions over 30 days, including: praying for an unchurched friend, completing a devotional guide, and inviting a friend to a special service. Through the devotional guide and the sermons, participants are taught how to be good friends, *as well as how to let Christ minister to others through their friendship.*

NOT JUST ANOTHER ATTENDANCE PROGRAM

How does the *Celebration of Friendship* differ from attendance programs?
1. Friends are not asked to sign a commitment to attend. Church members make the commitments.
2. The prayer and devotional life of church members is strengthened.

3. Church members are instructed in and perform steps in friendship evangelism.

Receive a complete planning guide customized to your dates. It includes:
    Explanation of the program strategy
    Decision guide to aid planning
    Announcements
    Phone scripts
    Letters
    Printing instructions

Five complete sermon manuscripts are included. Complete with:
    Major and minor points
    Illustrations
    Application

Also receive camera-ready, reproducible materials *customized with your church name and information*. Use them to produce:
    30 day devotional guide
    Bulletin inserts
    Bulletin blanks (8.5 x 11—both single fold and brochure fold
    masters are included)
    Invitation to the special service
    Commitment sheets
    Sermon note-taking bulletin inserts

For more information, or to place an order, visit http://grow.faithweb.com.

INDEX

JOT DOWN YOUR IDEAS HERE

JOT DOWN YOUR IDEAS HERE

JOT DOWN YOUR IDEAS HERE

JOT DOWN YOUR IDEAS HERE

CPSIA information can be obtained at www.ICGtesting.com
Printed in the USA
LVOW061112161112

307476LV00002B/6/A